SAVE THE YELLOW POPINJAY!

That's what all the cubs are saying about Bear Country's endangered bird. If Squire Grizzly gets his way and cuts down the trees in Birder's Woods, the popinjay will have nowhere to nest. Then it could disappear forever. It's up to the cubs to save it— before it's too late!

BIG CHAPTER BOOKS

The Berenstain Bears and the SHOWDOWN AT CHAINSAW GAP

by the Berenstains

A BIG CHAPTER BOOK™

Random House New York

Copyright © 1995 by Berenstain Enterprises, Inc.

Library of Congress Cataloging-in-Publication Data
Berenstain, Stan.
The Berenstain bears and the showdown at Chainsaw Gap /
by Stan and Jan Berenstain.
   p.   cm. — (A big chapter book)
SUMMARY: When Brother's class studies birds, the citizens of
Bear Country end up choosing sides in a battle between
environmentalists and those who want to cut down the trees in
Birder's Woods to build houses.
ISBN 0-679-87571-9 (pbk.) — ISBN 0-679-97571-3 (lib. bdg.)
[1. Birds—Fiction.   2. Environmental protection—Fiction.
3. School field trips—Fiction.   4. Schools—Fiction.
5. Bears—Fiction.]   I. Berenstain, Stan.   Big chapter book.
PZ7.B4483Beju   1995
[Fic]—dc20   95-8472

Manufactured in the United States of America   10 9 8 7 6 5 4 3 2 1

Contents

Chapter 1
The Almost War

The citizens of Bear Country usually got along very well with each other. They did have their differences, of course. Dogs barking and running loose sometimes caused arguments. When there were minor traffic accidents, folks might shout at each other until Officer Marguerite showed up. And the question of who owned the meadow between Squire Grizzly's estate and Farmer Ben's farm was the cause of trouble every now and then. But such problems were usually worked out without too much fuss.

How could it have happened, then, that Bear Country's peaceful, friendly citizens almost went to war against each other—neighbor against neighbor, husband against wife, cub against parent, boyfriend against girlfriend? All because of a creature that hatched from an egg not much bigger than a thimble—a creature that didn't weigh much more than a potato chip and that hardly anyone had ever heard of.

Sometimes trouble happens when things that don't seem to have anything to do with each other turn out to have *a lot* to do with each other. In this case, those things were a school assignment, a junkyard, and a big business deal.

It was a near thing, that almost war. It came to be known as…

THE SHOWDOWN AT CHAINSAW GAP!

Chapter 2
A Subject for the Birds

"Bertha, would you pass these out, please?"

Teacher Bob handed Bertha Broom a stack of papers. "These are the guides for a new study unit," he said as Bertha passed the papers out to the class. "I'm trying a new teaching approach with this unit, and

I'm very excited about it. We're going to take one subject and study every aspect of it before going on to something else. There will be classroom work and homework as usual. But there will also be special assignments. We might even have field studies and class trips."

What's the subject of this exciting new study unit? wondered the cubs. They took their guides from Bertha and looked eagerly at the heading. The subject was...*birds*.

Ferdy Factual and Trudy Brunowitz read their guides with great interest. But no one else read past the heading.

"Birds?" said Barry Bruin. He made a face and looked around at his classmates.

"Why birds?" said Bonnie Brown.

"What do *birds* have to do with anything?" moaned Queenie McBear.

"Why can't we have a unit on something

interesting—like dinosaurs?" said Brother Bear.

"Or space flight?" said Cousin Fred.

"Or poetry?" said Babs Bruno.

"Boy!" said Barry. "When Teacher Bob lays an egg, it's a *lulu!*"

Too-Tall Grizzly and his gang always made fun of new study units. Usually they did it just to annoy Teacher Bob. But this time they really looked upset.

"Birds!?" said Too-Tall. "Say it ain't so, Teach!"

The whole class groaned and moaned until...WHAP! Teacher Bob's yardstick came down hard across his desk.

"Quiet down, class," he said. "We've still got some time before recess, so let me try to make a point. You may *grouse* about this unit. But if any of you *turkeys* tries to *chicken* out of or *duck* this assignment, I'm

going to *goose* you hard, and you'll wind up eating *crow*."

Teacher Bob ended his speech with a big smile. It was the smile of someone proud of a great joke he's just made. But no one else seemed to know what the joke was.

No one except Ferdy Factual, that is. He stood and addressed the class. "Don't you get it? By using the names of six kinds of birds in a sentence, Teacher Bob has made an excellent point: that birds are an important part of our everyday lives!"

"Sit down, Ferdy," said Queenie.

"Without birds, our species could not survive," continued Ferdy. "Birds protect our food supply by eating millions of insect pests. And they do the necessary job of spreading plant seeds in their droppings…"

"If you don't shut up, you little nerd," growled Too-Tall from the back of the room, "I'm gonna drop *you!*"

"All right, Too-Tall, that's enough," said Teacher Bob. "What Ferdy has said is right, class. Birds *are* important. But what's more important for all of you to realize right now

is that we're going to study birds no matter how much you complain. So you'd all better start developing a positive attitude about it. Instead of moaning, why not think of ways to help our project? Any ideas?"

The cubs were quiet for a while. Then Cousin Fred raised his hand. "I could bring in my collection of birds' nests," he said.

"Excellent," said Teacher Bob. "Anyone else? Brother Bear?"

"Sister's got a neat collection of feathers," said Brother. "I could probably borrow it."

As the class discussed ideas for the project, Brother had a thought. Why not use the new study unit as a way to spend some extra time with Bonnie Brown? Quickly he wrote a note to Bonnie and passed it down his row.

Bonnie unfolded the note, but before she could read it she heard Teacher Bob clear

9

his throat loudly—"Ahem!" She looked up. Teacher Bob was staring straight at her. She knew he didn't approve of note passing in class.

"Why not share it with the whole class?" said Teacher Bob, taking the note from Bonnie. "After all, we're trying to work as a team on this new study unit."

Brother blushed as Teacher Bob read the note to himself.

"Hmm," said Teacher Bob. "It's from Brother Bear."

There were snickers from Too-Tall and the gang. Brother blushed harder.

"Brother suggests a bird walk in Birder's Woods this Saturday," said Teacher Bob.

Too-Tall and the gang made smooching noises. A few of the other cubs joined in. Brother blushed so hard his ears seemed to burn.

"Actually, that's a great suggestion for the whole class," said Teacher Bob. "It's a terrific way to kick off our new study unit. Thank you, Brother."

"Don't mention it," Brother muttered under his breath.

"I have a suggestion, too," said Ferdy. "How about a class trip to my Uncle Actual Factual's museum at the Bearsonian Institution? It has a great Hall of Birds."

Already the class's attitude was improving. A walk in Birder's Woods and a trip to the Hall of Birds sounded pretty good.

But not to Too-Tall and his gang.

"Hey, boss," said Skuzz. "Want me to shut the little bird lover up?"

"Maybe later in the schoolyard," said Too-Tall. "If we nail him here, Teach'll just send us to Grizzmeyer's office, and I can't afford another suspension anytime soon. My dad's still on the warpath from the last time."

The recess bell rang.

"Good," said Too-Tall. "I've never needed recess so bad in my life!"

As the cubs headed for the schoolyard, Barry Bruin hurried down the hallway to catch up to Babs Bruno. Babs had both hands full of blackboard erasers. It was her job that day to clean the erasers outside during recess.

"Hey, Babs," said Barry. "I've got a bird poem for you."

"Roses are red,
    Violets are blue.
    Storks have bird legs,
    And so do you!"

Barry ran on ahead of Babs. But he wasn't fast enough to escape the erasers she threw at him. Clouds of chalk dust rose as they bonked off his head.

Chapter 3
Thank You, Mr. G

Out in the schoolyard, Queenie McBear walked up to Too-Tall and winked at him. Too-Tall was a little surprised, because Queenie had been ignoring him lately.

"I expect to see you on that bird walk on Saturday," said Queenie.

Hmm, thought Too-Tall. *Looks like our on-again, off-again thing is on again.* That would make the bird walk a bit less painful. But he didn't want his gang to know he felt that way.

"Gimme a break, Queenie," he said. "I got better things to do on a Saturday morning than hang around with a bunch of stupid, boring birds."

"I couldn't help overhearing that remark," said Ferdy Factual, who was standing nearby with Trudy Brunowitz. "If you mean to say that birds lack value as a subject of study, then you are even lower on the bell curve of intelligence than I thought."

Too-Tall wasn't sure he'd been insulted. He looked at Queenie.

"He means you're dumber than he thought you were," she said.

15

Too-Tall glared at Ferdy. "I don't know anything about bell curves," he said. "But I do know how to make you *hear* bells—with *this!*" He raised one of his big fists and pushed it at Ferdy's face until it was almost touching his nose.

"Leave him alone!" said Trudy.

But Ferdy didn't seem to want any help. He looked Too-Tall right in the fist and said calmly, "I think it's only fair to warn you that Mr. Grizzmeyer is watching you from

his office window."

"Nice try," said Too-Tall. "But you're not gonna fool me with *that* old trick."

"Back off, big guy," said Queenie. "Mr. G *is* watching you from his office window. And if you get suspended again, your dad will ground you for the rest of the century. And if that happens, you won't be able to take me to the big dance. And if you don't take me to the big dance, you and I are finished...through...*splitsville!*"

Too-Tall's angry frown turned into a grin. "Hey, what's the problem?" he said. "I was just showing my little nerd buddy here this swollen knuckle."

"How did you get it?" said Ferdy. "Punching your way out of a paper bag?"

"Don't push your luck, nerdface," said Too-Tall. He put his big arm around Ferdy's narrow shoulders and sneaked a peek at the office window. Mr. G was gone. Too-Tall raised his fist again.

"Are you gonna pop him, boss?" asked Skuzz eagerly.

"Nah," said Too-Tall. "I'm gonna let him go."

"You're gonna *what*?" said Smirk.

"You heard me, birdbrain," said Too-Tall. "I'm gonna let him go…*if* he admits that

birds are boring and stupid. Go ahead, Ferdy, say it. *Birds are boring and stupid.* Say it!"

"I won't say it," said Ferdy bravely. "Because it isn't true. Birds are neither boring nor stupid. In fact, they are some of the most wonderful and interesting creatures on earth. The tiny cliff swallow, for example, flies seven thousand miles between its

summer and winter homes. The black-capped chickadee, with a brain even smaller than *yours*, can remember exactly where it found food the year before..."

"You *gotta* pop him now, boss!" said Vinnie.

Too-Tall needed no coaxing. Smiling wickedly, he drew back his mighty fist...

Just then there came a sudden shrill blast from a whistle. Too-Tall turned to see Mr. Grizzmeyer frowning at him from the front steps of the school building.

Instantly, Too-Tall opened his fist. He patted Ferdy on the shoulder. "A brain smaller than *mine?*" he said with a sweet smile. "How *interesting!*"

Chapter 4
Parts R Us

Across town from Bear Country School, the phone was ringing in the office of Too-Tall's dad, Two-Ton Grizzly. Two-Ton answered it.

"Hello, Parts R Us," he said. "If we ain't got it, we'll get it. Two-Ton speakin'. Cotter pins? Sure, we got cotter pins. Come on out. We're on the main road just past Birder's Woods, before you get to Buzzard Flats. You can't miss it."

Two-Ton was right. No one could have missed his place of business. It covered acres and acres of land. At the entrance was a huge sign that said PARTS R US. IF WE AIN'T GOT IT, WE'LL GET IT! From one end of the vast lot to the other lay piles of auto parts and wrecks of cars and trucks. Every day, folks came from miles around to look for fenders, bumpers, wheels, and other parts for all kinds of cars and trucks.

OFFICE

But it wasn't only the size of Two-Ton's business that caught folks' attention. His office was one of the most unusual around. It was a huge truck cab resting on piles of railroad ties. Two-Ton liked to sit in that office high above the wrecks and piles of parts and look out over the great stretch of land beyond. He especially enjoyed watching the buzzards soar and circle in the sky.

Two-Ton had always thought of that land out there as his own space. And he needed space—lots of it. He wore size "extra large," and he didn't like being crowded.

Behind Two-Ton's office was the family home, which was even stranger. It looked as if it were made of truck bodies welded together. That's because it *was* made of truck bodies welded together.

At first Two-Ton and his wife had lived in a single truck trailer. Then, as the family

grew, they added to their home. They added a bread truck when Too-Tall's older sister was born, then a U-Haul van when Too-Tall came along. Later, when business got better, they added another truck trailer.

The Grizzlys' family home may have been unusual, but it was no more unusual than the family itself. Too-Tall, of course, was known to all as the cub who held the record for times suspended from Bear Country School. His big sister, Too-Much, worked as a bouncer at a local bar and restaurant. And Two-Ton himself was the strongest bear in

TWO-TON

Too-Too

Beartown—strong enough to carry a whole truck engine on his shoulder.

But the most surprising member of the family was Two-Ton's wife, Too-Too. She was tiny compared with the rest of her family, but she was very much in charge of things.

Two-Ton's office phone rang again. "Hello, Parts R Us," said Two-Ton. "If we ain't got it, we'll get it. Hubcaps? Got loads of hubcaps. We're on the main road between Birder's Woods and Buzzard Flats. You can't miss it."

Just then something happened that Two-Ton couldn't miss. As he looked out over the stretch of land beyond Parts R Us, a

truck turned off the main road and drove out onto Buzzard Flats. The driver and a helper took some posts and a sign from the back of the truck. They drove the posts into the ground and nailed the sign to them. Then they backed the truck off Buzzard Flats and came rolling down the road toward Parts R Us.

As the truck passed Two-Ton's office, he could clearly read the words printed on its side. They said BEARTOWN CONSTRUCTION COMPANY.

Two-Ton frowned. He didn't like the looks of this.

He climbed down from his office, walked between the wrecks and piles of parts, and headed out onto Buzzard Flats for a look at the sign. When he reached it, his heart sank.

The sign said:

The Future Site of
COZY CORNER COTTAGES
A Lovely Community of
447 Fine Homes

Chapter 5
A Gift from the Squire

Back on the other side of town, Brother and Sister Bear were just getting home from school.

"Okay," said Sister as they walked down the sunny dirt road. "I'll lend you my feather collection if you'll let Lizzy and me come along on the Saturday bird walk."

"I'm sure Teacher Bob won't mind," said Brother. "Come on! Race you to the house!" Brother took off.

"No fair!" yelled Sister, running to catch up. "You had a head start!"

The cubs found Mama in the kitchen having a cup of tea with Papa, who was taking a break from his work.

"Hi, cubs," said Mama. "How was school?"

"Tell you later," said Brother as he headed for the living room.

Sister told her parents about the upcoming bird walk.

AH, BIRDER'S WOODS . . .

"Ah, Birder's Woods...," said Papa, leaning back in his chair with his hands clasped behind his head. "Wonderful place. Your mother and I used to take long walks there before we were married. That woods has belonged to Squire Grizzly's family for generations."

In the living room, Brother was searching for something in the bookcase. "Hey!" he called. "I have to look up *birds* in the encyclopedia. Where's the 'B' book?"

"Out in my shop," Papa called back. "I had to look up *box elder*. Squire Grizzly is giving me the wood from some box elder trees he cut down. I wanted to find out what it's good for."

The kitchen phone rang, and Mama answered. "Speaking of the squire," she said to Papa, "he wants to talk to you."

Papa was still on the phone with Squire Grizzly when Brother returned from the workshop and began reading about birds in the encyclopedia. Through the kitchen door, Mama could see him sprawled out on the living room sofa.

"Your brother seems pretty excited about this new study unit," she said to Sister.

"What he's excited about is going for a walk in the woods with Bonnie Brown," said Sister.

"Hush, you two—this is important!" said Papa. "Yes, Squire. I understand. You want to see me at your office downtown at three o'clock Wednesday. I'll be there." Papa hung up and looked at Mama.

"What was that all about?" asked Mama.

"I don't know," said Papa. "All he said was that it was important."

Mama rose and went to the stove. "Time

to set the table, cubs," she said. "Dinner's almost ready."

The cubs got out the dishes and silverware and began setting the table. But Brother seemed to be daydreaming. That must have been why he bumped into Sister.

"Hey, watch out!" said Sister. "I already set that place!"

"Sorry, Sis," said Brother. "By the way, did you know that birds have hollow bones? Being so light helps them fly. And their wing muscles are super-powerful—as strong as a lion's jaw muscles..."

"You aren't going to dazzle Bonnie with that kind of talk," said Sister. "What you need is some juicy stuff about *lovebirds*."

"That's enough teasing, Sister," said Mama. "And, Brother, mind what you're doing. The knives and spoons go on the *right*, and the forks go on the *left*."

"Sorry, Mama," said Brother.

Meanwhile, Papa was standing by the phone, scratching his head. "Hmm," he said softly, more to himself than to his family. "I wonder what the Squire has in mind...."

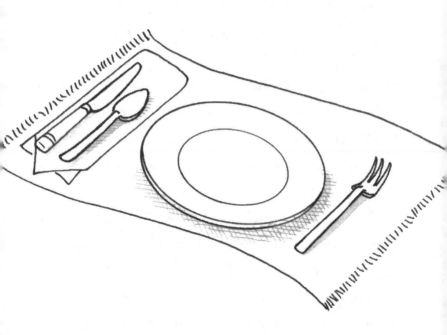

Chapter 6
In Birder's Woods

When Saturday came, Teacher Bob and his class, along with Sister Bear and Lizzy Bruin, met at Bear Country School to catch the bus to Birder's Woods.

Teacher Bob organized the cubs into bird-watching teams. Brother and Bonnie convinced him to let them be a team all on their own. So did Ferdy Factual and Trudy Brunowitz.

Those were the only twosome teams. Queenie and Too-Tall were almost a twosome, though, because the other gang members had orders from Too-Tall to walk at least five yards behind him whenever he was with Queenie.

In spite of themselves, many of the cubs were excited about the bird walk. Some had binoculars, and a few carried cameras. Bertha Bruin even brought a minicam. In fact, on the way to Birder's Woods, only Too-Tall and his gang joked and snickered about the new study unit.

"All right, quiet down, everyone," said Teacher Bob as the bus pulled to a stop at the woods. "Before we begin, I have some instructions for you bird watchers."

In the back of the bus, Too-Tall and Skuzz made chirping noises while Smirk and Vinnie flapped their arms.

"That'll be enough, guys," said Teacher Bob. "Which brings me to the first instruction: *Be quiet in the woods*. If you're noisy,

you won't see any birds. Second instruction: If you see a bird whose name you know, write it down on your list. If you don't know the name, check it out in my big bird book here." He held up a huge book that must have had at least a thousand pages. "Or talk to Ferdy or Trudy—they have bird guides in their heads."

The teams entered the woods, being careful to keep some distance apart. It was early May, and the trees were full of new leaves. Before long, the cubs were spotting all sorts of birds. Cardinals, blue jays, sparrows, and starlings were noted on the bird watchers' lists.

Brother had been looking forward to his walk in the woods with Bonnie. But now he wasn't sure why. Bonnie was acting as if he wasn't even there at all. Several times he tried to get her to look at a bird he had spotted. But she kept her eyes on the ground in front of her. She seemed lost in thought.

Finally Brother tapped her on the arm and said, "What's on your mind, Bonnie?"

Brother could tell that she had heard him, but she didn't answer right away. Then she said softly, "This is such a pretty place. It's a shame that…" Suddenly she stopped speaking.

"It's a shame that what?" asked Brother.

"Oh, nothing," said Bonnie. Just then she noticed something overhead. "Hey, isn't that a wood thrush?" she asked, pointing.

Not far behind them, Queenie had just

found a blue robin's egg on the ground.

"Look at this, Too-Tall," she said, holding it up. "I found it in this soft patch of grass. It must have fallen from a nest."

"Give it here," said Too-Tall. "Bet I can hit the trunk of that tree over there with it."

"You'll do no such thing!" said Queenie angrily.

Too-Tall shrugged. "I'd take it home and scramble it for lunch, but it's too little."

"Oh, Too-Tall!" cried Queenie. "Look. It's not even broken. If we can find the nest, we can put it back. Hey, there's the nest over in that bush."

Too-Tall leaned down to look over Queenie's shoulder as she gently placed the egg back in its nest, where it rested with four other blue eggs.

"There," she said. "Now the baby bird can hatch along with its brothers and sisters."

Too-Tall stared at the eggs in the nest. "Wow," he said. "You mean birds are gonna come out of those little eggs?"

"Of course, you big lug," said Queenie. "What did you think's going to come out of them—egg salad?"

Too-Tall just kept staring in wonderment.

The rest of the gang came over for a closer look. "What's takin' so long, boss?" asked Skuzz.

"Back off, you jerks!" barked Too-Tall. "You wanna frighten 'em?"

Skuzz gave Too-Tall a puzzled look. "How are we gonna frighten *eggs?*" he said.

"Never mind that," said Too-Tall.

Just then Too-Tall spied a robin on the ground not far away. It ran back and forth, dragging one of its wings along the ground. "Hey, look!" he said. "That must be the mother. And she has a broken wing!"

As Too-Tall's team watched the robin, Ferdy and Trudy came up behind them. "What did you find?" asked Trudy.

"A mother robin with a broken wing!" said Too-Tall. He sounded worried.

"Oh, she's only *pretending* that her wing is broken," said Ferdy. "She's acting."

"What do we look like—talent scouts?" said Smirk.

"She thinks you might want to harm her eggs," Trudy explained. "So she's trying to distract you. She wants to make you forget about the nest. Lots of different kinds of birds do that."

"Wow...," said Too-Tall. He stared at the mother robin for a long time.

"Hey, Too-Tall," said Queenie finally. "Say something. What's wrong with you?"

"Oh, he's fine," said Ferdy with a chuckle. "He's just beginning to realize that birds aren't as boring and stupid as he thought."

Chapter 7
The Hall of Shame

On Monday and Tuesday, Teacher Bob's class worked on their written reports of their walk in Birder's Woods. Then, on Wednesday, they went on their class trip to the Hall of Birds at the Bearsonian Institution.

Professor Actual Factual was their guide. First he showed them an exhibit about the history of birds. There were fossils to see and charts showing how birds had arisen from other winged creatures millions of years ago.

Then the professor took them into the section about birds of today. All around the great room were exhibits of birds. Each type of bird was in a special display, with a large window in front and a mural covering the walls behind. Professor Actual Factual explained that the murals were paintings of the birds' natural habitats.

"What's a *habitat*?" asked Barry Bruin.

"I'm glad you asked that question," said the professor. But before he could answer, Cousin Fred's hand shot up. Fred not only read the dictionary for fun, but he seemed to remember every word in it. "All right, Fred," said the professor. "Give it a try."

"Habitat," said Fred. *"The natural environment of a plant or animal, containing everything it needs for its survival and reproduction."*

"Right you are," said the professor.

As they walked slowly around the room, Actual Factual told them about the natural habitat and way of life of each kind of bird they saw. There were birds from forests, fields, rivers, lakes, and oceans. There were birds that could run fast but couldn't fly, like the ostrich. There were birds, like the penguin, that couldn't fly but could swim and dive. There were birds that ate seeds, birds that ate fruit, birds that ate insects, birds that ate fish.

"I know what kind of fish birds eat, professor," said Barry Bruin.

"You do?" said Actual Factual. "All right, what kind?"

"*Flying* fish!"

Half of the cubs laughed. The other half just groaned.

"Ah, yes, a witticism. Quite amusing, Barry," said the professor. "But now I'm afraid I must lead you to an exhibit that isn't funny at all. It's called the Hall of Shame."

The Hall of Shame? thought the cubs. What could be on display *there?*

The exhibit was in a little alcove off the main hall. On display were life-size models of three birds. The first was labeled DODO. The second was labeled PASSENGER PIGEON.

And the third was labeled YELLOW POPINJAY. On the wall behind them was a sign that said EXTINCT! GONE FOREVER!

Again Cousin Fred's hand shot up. But Actual Factual motioned for him to put it down.

"Let me handle this one," said the professor. "*Extinct* means exactly what it says there on the sign: *gone forever*. There are no living dodos, passenger pigeons, or yellow popinjays left anywhere in the world. Many kinds of animals have become extinct over the years, and many more are in danger of becoming extinct soon. The most important cause of extinction is the loss of natural habitat..."

Most of the cubs listened closely to Actual Factual's talk on extinction. Many had never heard of extinction and were surprised that an animal could disappear completely from the face of the earth—forever.

But one cub had stopped listening. That cub was Bertha Broom. She had a puzzled frown on her face. Finally she raised her hand. But Actual Factual didn't notice her.

Teacher Bob leaned down to Bertha and whispered, "I'm sure the professor will answer questions when he's finished talking."

The instant Actual Factual asked for questions, Bertha's hand shot back up.

"Yes, Bertha," said the professor.

"There's something I don't understand," she said. "If the yellow popinjay is extinct, then how come I saw one in Birder's Woods last Saturday morning?"

For a moment Actual Factual stared at Bertha with raised eyebrows. Then he tried to smile. "Oh, another joke," he said.

"Everyone knows, of course, that the yellow popinjay has been extinct for seventy-five years. Really, Bertha, I don't think it's proper to make jokes like that here in the Hall of Shame."

"But I'm *not* joking," said Bertha. "I saw one, and I can prove it."

"You must have seen some other yellow

I SAW ONE, AND I CAN PROVE IT.

bird," said the professor. "It's easy for a beginning bird watcher to make such a mistake. You probably saw a sulfur titmouse, a yellow-bellied sapsucker, or a..." The professor stopped short and looked straight at Bertha. "What do you mean when you say you can *prove* it?"

"I mean just *that*," said Bertha. "I got it on my minicam. It wasn't in Teacher Bob's book, and Ferdy didn't know what it was. He said to show it to you. Here's the cassette."

"Excellent," said Actual Factual. "Since you have it on tape, we can find out exactly what kind of bird it is. This will be a good lesson on bird watching, cubs. It's so easy to be fooled."

The professor led the group into his office and popped the cassette into the VCR.

"Whatever it is," Ferdy said to Teacher Bob, "Uncle Actual will recognize it instantly. He knows even more about birds than *I* do."

A tiny yellow bird came into focus on the

screen. It was pecking at some berries on a bush. The moment the professor saw it, his mouth fell open and his jaw dropped. "I don't believe it!" he gasped. "A *yellow popinjay!* I simply don't believe it!"

"Seeing *is* believing, Professor," said Bertha.

The professor rushed to the screen. He all but put his nose against it. "But what's that it's eating? *Bugleberries!* It's eating bugleberries! Birder's Woods is *full* of bugleberry bushes...."

Actual Factual dashed to the bookshelf and took down a book called *Birds of the Past*. He thumbed through it hurriedly. "Ah, here it is. Why, yes...bugleberries were the yellow popinjay's main food before it became extinct." He stared again at the TV screen, where the yellow bird continued pecking at the small red berries. "Or maybe I should say—before it was *thought* to be extinct!"

The professor switched off the TV and held out his hand to Teacher Bob. "Congratulations to you and your class!" he said with a broad smile. "Because of your study unit on birds, a great scientific discovery has been made!"

Chapter 8
He's My Uncle,
and I Love Him!

The cubs buzzed with excitement as they rode the bus back to school. What a discovery! A bird that everyone thought had been extinct for nearly a century!

But one cub didn't seem excited at all. That cub was Bonnie Brown. Brother, who was sitting next to her, couldn't understand why she looked so gloomy. She didn't talk or smile. All she did was stare out the window.

Finally Brother said, "What's wrong, Bonnie? Come on, you can tell me."

For a while Bonnie said nothing. Then she turned to Brother. "Remember last Saturday in Birder's Woods?" she said. "When I started to say something and stopped?"

"Sure," said Brother. "What about it?"

"I was going to say that Birder's Woods is such a beautiful place that it's a shame Uncle Squire is going to cut it down."

"Cut it down?" said Brother. "Why?"

"He wants to use the wood for the houses he's going to build on Buzzard Flats."

"That would be a *terrible* thing to do!" said Brother. "It would be...*greedy* and *mean!* He can't do that! He just can't!"

"I don't see why not," said Bonnie angrily. "It's his woods. Uncle *owns* it. I guess he can cut it down if he wants to. And he is *not* greedy and mean! He's sweet and nice. He's my uncle, and I love him!"

"But Birder's Woods is the home of the yellow popinjay, a bird that's been extinct for seventy-five years!" cried Brother.

"Well, it's not extinct anymore," said Bonnie.

"But your uncle will be helping to *make* it extinct if he destroys this one's home," said Brother. "After all, if folks thought the yel-

low popinjay was extinct for seventy-five years, there can't be many left!"

"Well, what about the folks who will live in the houses that Uncle wants to build? What about *their* homes?" said Bonnie. "Besides, there's tons of other woods!"

"There's also tons of other places to get wood for building houses," said Brother. "You heard what the professor said about habitat. Don't you understand?"

"I understand, all right. I understand that you think my family is greedy and mean!"

Brother and Bonnie were so angry with each other that they didn't speak another word all the way back to school.

Finally, as the bus pulled into the parking lot, Brother said, "Will you at least tell your uncle about the yellow popinjay? *Please?*"

Bonnie just shrugged and looked away. "I'll think about it," she said.

Chapter 9
Choosing Sides

News of the discovery of the yellow popinjay spread quickly through Bear Country School. By the time Brother and Sister met in the hall to walk home together, everyone seemed to know about it.

"What a surprise!" said Sister as they headed home. "An extinct bird—alive and well!"

"I've got another surprise for you," said Brother gloomily. "The yellow popinjay may be alive, but it isn't well."

"What do you mean?" said Sister.

Brother told her about Squire Grizzly's plan to cut down Birder's Woods.

"Let's tell Mama and Papa right away," said Sister. "I'll bet they can think of a way to save the yellow popinjay."

But the cubs had yet another surprise when they got home. They found Papa in the kitchen talking excitedly to Mama. He greeted them with a big grin.

"Great news, cubs!" he said. "I just had my meeting with Squire Grizzly. He's going to build more than four hundred homes on Buzzard Flats. And I'll be in charge of the

whole job! We're going to use Birder's Woods for lumber. We'll start cutting it down Saturday morning."

"But, Papa! You can't do that!" cried Brother.

"Not all by myself, of course," said Papa. "I've already lined up a chainsaw crew. We'll have that woods down in nothing flat."

Brother quickly told his parents about the yellow popinjay. Mama looked worried. So did Papa—but only a little.

"It's too bad about this yellow whatchamacallit," he said. "But a deal's a deal. Besides, we're talking about more than four hundred homes. That means lots of jobs for my fellow members of the Association of Woodsbears."

"But it isn't just the yellow popinjay," said Brother. "Plenty of other creatures have their homes in Birder's Woods."

"Oh, they'll find new homes," said Papa.

"Not the yellow popinjay!" said Brother. "Where else in Bear Country are there so many bugleberry bushes? Think of the dodo and the passenger pigeon!"

"I never met any Mr. Dodo," said Papa. "And as far as I know, pigeons don't take passengers..."

"No, Papa!" cried Sister. "The dodo and the passenger pigeon are *extinct!*"

"Well, I'm sorry about Mr. Dodo and his pigeon pals. But the way I look at it, it's a case of this yellow popinbird versus hundreds of houses and gobs of jobs."

"Papa-a-a!" cried the cubs together.

Mama raised her hands for quiet. "I think we'd all better calm down before continuing this discussion," she said.

"What's the use?" said Brother. "Papa won't even listen! Let's go, Sis."

The cubs marched upstairs and began calling their friends on the phone. They soon found out that arguments about Birder's Woods were going on in lots of other families, too.

But arguments were only the first step. Queenie McBear and her mother were already hard at work organizing a demonstration against cutting down Birder's

Woods. According to their plan, dozens of citizens would show up at Birder's Woods on Saturday morning to stop Papa and his chainsaw crew.

Queenie and Ms. McBear convinced

quite a few grownups to be on their side, including Teacher Bob, Teacher Jane, and Dr. Gert Grizzly. But others were against the demonstration. Cousin Fred's dad, who was a lawyer, thought it might be against the law. Babs Bruno's dad, Police Chief Bruno, said he might even have to arrest the demonstrators for trespassing on Squire

Grizzly's property. And Biff Bruin, Barry and Lizzy's dad, said that any kind of trouble was bad for business.

Later that night, Brother got a call from Queenie.

"Guess what!" she said. "We've got five more demonstrators! Too-Tall and the gang are on our side!"

"Great!" said Brother. "But that's only four. Who's the fifth?"

"You'll never guess," said Queenie. "It's Too-Tall's dad."

"Two-Ton?" said Brother. "Wow! He could probably stop a chainsaw gang all by himself. Funny—I never pictured Two-Ton Grizzly as a bird lover."

"Oh, he doesn't care about the yellow popinjay," said Queenie. "But he cares a whole lot about keeping Cozy Corner Cottages out of his 'space.' Well, gotta go."

As Brother hung up, he noticed that Sister looked upset. "What's wrong, Sis?" he asked. "Are you scared of being in a demonstration?"

"It's not that," said Sister. "But a demonstration against *Papa?* He's so excited about getting that big job..."

"I feel bad about it too, Sis," said Brother. "Just think of it this way. Papa will get another big job sooner or later no matter what he does about Birder's Woods. But if he cuts it down, the yellow popinjay could be *gone forever*."

Sister nodded. But now Brother looked upset. "What's the matter?" she asked. "Afraid we'll get arrested?"

"It's not that," said Brother. "It's Bonnie. She's *really* mad at me."

"So call her up," said Sister. "Try to smooth things over."

Brother glanced at the phone. "Maybe you're right," he said.

Lady Grizzly answered the phone at Grizzly Mansion and went to get Bonnie. In a minute she was back. "I'm sorry, Brother," she said. "Bonnie refuses to come to the phone. What's going on between you two?"

Brother told her about the argument over Birder's Woods.

"Birder's Woods, you say," said Lady Grizzly. "Hmm. That's the first I've heard about it...."

Chapter 10
The Big Showdown

Thursday and Friday seemed to fly by as the bears of Beartown argued about Birder's Woods and busied themselves with making protest and anti-protest signs.

Saturday came in a hurry. Shortly after dawn, the main road along the edge of Birder's Woods was lined with bears. On one side, with their backs to the woods, stood Teacher Bob's class and a handful of other protesters. They held signs that said SAVE THE YELLOW POPINJAY!, REMEMBER THE DODO!, and THE SPECIES YOU SAVE MAY BE YOUR OWN! Along the other side of the road, facing the woods, were Papa Bear with his chainsaw crew and their support-

ers. Papa's crew carried heavy chainsaws, and their supporters held signs that said UP WITH WOODSBEARS, DOWN WITH TREE HUGGERS, and BEARS, NOT BIRDS!

Brother Bear wasn't really surprised to see Bonnie Brown standing with the chainsaw crew, holding a sign that said LOYAL TO MY UNCLE! But Brother—and everyone else—was very surprised to see who had joined the protesters.

Looking sideways down the line of protesters, Brother tapped Cousin Fred on the arm. "Hey, isn't that Lady Grizzly?" he said.

"Couldn't be," said Fred. But as he looked, his mouth opened in surprise. "It *is* Lady Grizzly!" he said. "And she's carrying a sign that says PROUD TO BE A TREE HUGGER!"

But the biggest shock of all was for Two-Ton Grizzly.

"Hey, Pop," said Too-Tall. "Look who's on the other side."

Two-Ton took a look and gasped. "Why, it's…it's…"

"That's right, Pop," said Too-Tall. "It's Mom and Sis."

Two-Ton couldn't believe his eyes. And he couldn't believe the sign Too-Too was carrying. It said COZY CORNER COTTAGES, HERE I COME!

"But, Sweetie," cried Two-Ton. "How can you do this to me?"

"Easy!" shouted Too-Too. "I'm tired of livin' in a dump! I wanna live in one of them Cozy Corner Cottages!"

"Me too, Daddy!" called Too-Much. "I'm sick of furniture with seat belts!"

"But why didn't you say something?" said Two-Ton.

"I'm sayin' it now, buster," said Too-Too. "So *live* with it!"

Two-Ton looked as if somebody had let the air out of him.

Down the line of protesters, Brother and Sister Bear were looking across the street at Papa. It wasn't easy going against their own father.

"We've got to stand firm," said Brother. "The yellow popinjay is counting on us!"

"Where's Mama?" asked Sister. "I don't see her anywhere."

"She must have stayed home," said Brother. "Probably couldn't make up her mind which side to be on. No one loves nature's creatures more than she does. But no one loves it more than Mama when Papa gets a big job, either."

Across the road, Papa Bear was looking back at Brother and Sister. He didn't like going against his own cubs. But he had a job to do.

"Out of the way!" he shouted to the pro-testers. "We're coming across to cut down those woods!"

"Stand your ground!" Queenie shouted up and down the line of protesters.

"This is your last warning!" called Papa.

The protesters didn't budge.

With a lump in his throat, Papa turned to his crew. "All right," he said. "Let's make a run at them. When you get past them, start your saws and head straight for the trees. Get ready...get set..."

But before Papa could yell "Go!" he heard something that made him pause.

Bonnie Brown heard it too. "What's that whirring sound?" she said.

"It's getting closer," said Papa. "And it's coming from the sky...."

Now everyone could hear the *put-put-put-put*. They all looked up at once.

It was a helicopter!

As the big helicopter came slowly down toward the road, a bullhorn poked out of one of the windows.

"This is the police!" boomed Chief Bruno's voice through the bullhorn. "Back away from the road, everyone! We're going to land!"

SAVE THE YELLOW POPINJAY!

SAVE

Chapter 11
A Change of Heart

The two lines of bears pulled back from the road. As the helicopter landed, the wind from its rotor blades raised a huge cloud of dust. Signs on both sides were blown every which way.

The door of the helicopter opened, and steps were let down to the ground.

"It looks like Chief Bruno decided not to arrest us," said Brother to Sister.

"How do you know?" asked Sister.

"If he came to arrest us, he'd bring a bunch of paddy wagons, not a helicopter," said Brother.

And, indeed, it did look as though Chief Bruno had something else in mind. For it wasn't just Officer Marguerite who followed him out of the helicopter. Out came Mayor Honeypot, Squire Grizzly, Professor Actual Factual, and—to everyone's surprise—Mama Bear!

Mayor Honeypot took the bullhorn from Chief Bruno and cleared his throat. The mayor had a way of mixing up the beginnings of his words, and this time was no exception.

"Sellow fitizens," he said. "Er, fellow citizens! Quire Squizzly—er, Squire Grizzly—has something to tell you!"

Squire Grizzly took the bullhorn. "You probably all know what a stubborn old coot I am," he said. "I want to thank my dear wife, Lady Grizzly, for opening my eyes about the yellow popinjay. Birder's Woods will stand. I'm giving it to the bears—and birds—of Bear Country...forever!"

A cheer went up from the protesters. They waved their signs with glee. But the chainsaw crew and its supporters didn't move a muscle. They were stunned.

Squire Grizzly raised his hands for quiet.

"But that doesn't mean we aren't going to build Cozy Corner Cottages," he said. "We will! All four hundred plus! I'll buy the wood from Big Bear City Lumber Company. And there will be plenty of work for all you woodsbears!"

A cheer went up from Papa's chainsaw crew and their supporters.

"What about the yellow popinjay?" shouted Bertha Broom when the cheering had died down. "Is he safe?"

Professor Actual Factual took the bull-horn. "She—I repeat, *she*—is quite safe," he said. "As soon as I heard about the squire's plan to cut down Birder's Woods, I moved her to my bird refuge across town.

And I am pleased to announce that she has
just laid four eggs! There are only a few
bugleberry bushes at the refuge. But for the
time being they will provide enough food
for the mother, as well as for her babies
when they hatch. As soon as the babies are
old enough, I will move them and their

mother back to their natural habitat in Birder's Woods, where they can eat bugle-berries to their hearts' content. Now I will ask Mama Bear to say a few words. Mama?"

Mama shook her head. She refused to take the bullhorn from Actual Factual.

"Mama Bear is much too modest," said Actual Factual. "But I must tell you, it was Mama who saved the day. It was she who went to Mayor Honeypot and explained that, while there may not be two sides to *every* question, there are definitely two sides to *this* one. So let's hear it for Mama Bear!"

Mama got the biggest cheer of all.

When the helicopter took off to head back to town, Mama stayed behind. She motioned for Papa and the cubs to come together with her for a big family hug.

"Phew!" said Papa. "I'm sure glad that's

over! Now I can get back to my carpentry work. Being in charge of a whole big job wasn't any fun. Too much excitement, too many phone calls, too many papers to fill out."

Brother went over to Bonnie and held out his hand. "I'm sorry about the argument we had," he said.

"Me, too," said Bonnie. "Let's be friends again."

They shook hands. Soon they were talking happily, just like old times.

Chapter 12
Home, Sweet Home

Before long, four little yellow popinjays hatched from Mother Popinjay's eggs. As soon as they were old enough to be moved, Professor Actual Factual put them and their mother in a bugleberry bush in the deepest, safest part of Birder's Woods.

The "almost war" over the yellow popinjay was long remembered in Bear Country. And so were the lessons it taught. The main lesson was that, as often as not, there are two sides to every question—even tough ones.

Over the next few months, Cozy Corner Cottages was built on Buzzard Flats. And

Two-Ton Grizzly, high up in his truck-cab office, learned to live with more than four hundred houses sitting in his "space." He even learned to like living in one of them. For, as it turned out, Two-Ton was tired of living in a dump, too.

Stan and Jan Berenstain began writing and illustrating books for children in the early 1960s, when their two young sons were beginning to read. That marked the start of the best-selling Berenstain Bears series. Now, with more than one hundred books in print, videos, television shows, and even Berenstain Bears attractions at major amusement parks, it's hard to tell where the Bears end and the Berenstains begin!

Stan and Jan make their home in Bucks County, Pennsylvania, near their sons—Leo, a writer, and Michael, an illustrator—who are helping them with Big Chapter Books stories and pictures. They plan on writing and illustrating many more books for children, especially for their four grand-children, who keep them well in touch with the kids of today.